I Heard Her Say

———

MontyQuinn

Copyright © 2017 by Wet Ink Publishing

All rights reserved. No part of this book may be reproduced or transmitted in any form or by any means without written permission from the author.

ISBN 978-0-9988326-0-9

Cover Design: James Bates III for Crush Imaging Studios

Editor: Desiree Edmonson

Dedication

This book is dedicated to my kids; **Qi'Moni** and **Quinlan**. Without you guys I don't know where I would be. God blessed me to be your father and I will go to my grave trying to be the best daddy that I can be. You two are the greatest gifts that have ever been given to me!!! And to my wife **Jade**, you have stretched me in ways that I never knew I could stretch. Because of you I am better.

I also dedicate this book to my friend, my PlayaPartna; **Rayco Campbell**. Much of this book was written while I had a first-hand seat witnessing you battle and defeat cancer. Your fight helped bring my life into great perspective. Our talks were priceless and the experience of walking by your side through your most trying time showed me that these little things that are made into big things are simply distractions used to remove the smile that you kept throughout your life's most trying time. I will never forget you and your impact on my life. **#TeamRayco4Life**

Foreword

  I met Quincey in a Facebook group where we would exchange ideas and thoughts. I would share one of my original poems and in what seemed like a matter of minutes, he would have a poetic response to it. I was always flattered that he would take the time to write something in return to something that I had written. It was as if he heard me say several different things through some of my own poetry. I would share with him some of my work before I would share them with anyone else because I valued his opinion of it.

  He had mentioned to me that he was writing a book. He shared a poem with me that he was considering putting in the book. I was honored to have been able to read his works and talk with him about how they made me feel or what I thought it meant. He would ask me every day, "are you writing?" Oftentimes my response was no. I was dry. I had a block that could not be moved, but he continued to push me. One day I woke up and out of nowhere I began to write again. The process of sharing my works with him continued and vice versa.

  I am proud of my friend for taking the time to listen to us as women. To hear what we are saying. To be an active participant in the ongoing conversation that men and women have. He heard us say a lot from what we want in our man to how hurt from a mother's departure still lingers. Whatever the emotion, it is captured in the lines of verse in this collection. I am no expert but I am proud of the work he has done!

Nanci Mays

Introduction

Ladies, I love talking to you, experiencing your experiences in the most personal and honest ways, seeking to understand your thoughts and emotions by walking down your mental hallways. I seek to know you better, so I listen intently every time you speak to share your heart. I am amazed by the stories of strength and courage during the times life had seemed to have fallen apart. I relish in your accomplishments; success exposes another facet of your complexity all be it simple in nature. Every level of emotion must be observed to truly identify with a woman's behavior. I cannot say that I have yet made it in the room but I am comfortable standing and listening from the doorway. I hope you enjoy reading what I Heard Her Say!

Playing Games

I am well past the age that I am interested in playing any games with a man. I came to this conclusion long ago after experiencing how hurtful games can afflict the heart firsthand. Half a century of experience has taught me many lessons in dealing with the matters of the heart. Still I find myself falling in love with men who only leave my heart torn apart. Married twice, I really don't want failed relationships to continue to be a part of my life. I have a lot to offer and even more that I would love to give. I am only looking for someone who is trustworthy, caring and appreciative. It makes no sense to me why men over forty-five have so much uncertainty regarding relationship. It is as if they are trying to relive their past instead of settling down into commitment. It is the same old pattern; in the beginning, everything is lovely and great. Then once you make love to them, being in a relationship becomes the great debate. They suddenly become busy; never mind the fact that they were with you every day for the last ninety days. They expect you to believe that they care, as you watch the rapid change in their once attentive ways. Paying no mind to how much your feeling's have evolved based on their false actions. How you're left hurt with nothing but questions concerning their sudden detachment. I cannot explain how much it hurts to be left with nothing but unanswered questions about a situation that you care so much about. It becomes a part of your life that you are left alone to figure out. You find yourself having lonely moments that turn into lonelier days and nights. Pondering the situations as it stands and what it is that you did not do right. The situation overall weighs heavy on the heart and is very stressful to the mind. Craziest part of it all is that when you finally get over things you realize that you have wasted precious time.

I Heard Her Say

I have painfully heard his explanation,
I now overflow with frustration.
Hearing him speak of how he fell into temptation;
Instead of staying at home and fulfilling his marital obligations,
Now I'm sitting here with the heartbreaking realization,
That there has just been a painful shift in my situation

My admiration has been turned into a feeling of stagnation,
What was once a feeling of total elation
Is now just a numbing sensation.
Sexual infatuation is the cause of our relationship's termination
He couldn't resist the hooker's invitation
Now he has nothing;
That is a steep price to pay in my estimation

Really, where was the gratification?
Did it fulfil your fascination?
Now because of your participation in fornication
Your pleasure is yours alone.
Masturbation

How could you? What is your justification?
I hope it was worth our love's nullification

For your acts, there will be ramifications
My lawyer is in the process of breaking down all the calculations
Due to your deviation my concentration is on a new destination
One where there is much celebration and admiration
I am to be appreciated with nothing less than love and dedication

However, you have provided me painful education
That has led to my graduation
And after much deliberation;
For you, I have nothing but appreciation
Your faults have provided me revelation
Your infatuation has led to my emancipation
Let all those bearing witness say...Liberation!!!

So in the end I have decided that there will be no retaliation
I have gone through my emotional recuperation and rejuvenation
And upon further investigation

I came to the conclusion that because of much procrastination
And the fear to have an adult conversation
We both are responsible for the devastation that we are facing.

So I will take my compensation as a consolation
Thanking you for the process of maturation
Seeing this less as a blow to my foundation
Just tribulation that provides future motivation
This is nothing but human transformation
I have actually gained stabilization through your self-elimination.

Dumbfounded

When you left; you did it with your head held high.
You had no explanation, no remorse and your ears had fallen deaf to my cry.
You simply just walked away....
I did not get a call;
A text;
An apology;
I made a mistake.
I gave you everything and in the end you left me with heartbreak.
You left without reason, not even the excuse, "I need my space."
Confusion clouded my heart and mind and was revealed in the bewildered expression I wore on my face.
I was literally dumbfounded by your actions; how does one react to such an empty deed?
What are the next steps in this journey and how do I proceed?
You left me lonely to wallow in my own despair.
When I needed you the most; you were not there.
I had no clue as to why I was hurting, I just knew I was. I was conflicted within because you walked away with my love.

Dumbfounded…

And so now you return….
Returning to a place you claim that you should have never left.
With proclamation that no one can do you like I can; all of a sudden I am what is best.
Now you want forever but it was not too long ago I did not warrant a reason for your sudden exit.
How am I to know that you finally appreciate me as a blessing?
I have given you countless chances and you have said nothing at all.
You could not convince me of your change of heart even if you got down on your knees and crawled.
How do you expect me to forgive an action I still don't understand?
All I know is that this is getting out of hand.
I am dumbfounded; completely speechless and amazed
And above all else I feel abandoned and betrayed

Who Can I Run To?

Who can I run to now that this man has destroyed my heart and stymied my ability to love?
I am left with tattooed tears, an unwillingness to trust, and an undying pain that I cannot get rid of.
Him walking out on me constantly replays in my mind even when I sleep.
How do you erase traumatic memories when they are buried in your soul so deep?
I am broken; held prisoner by my pain,
Unable to make sense of the situation; I am so lost and ashamed.
Afraid to move forward; this situation has left me unsure of myself,
I gave him all that I had and he left, so what good am I to anyone else?
I just want to hide so that no one can see the emotional state that I am in,
I trusted him with my life and he left me for my best friend.
Tell me who can I run to, now that my life has been fractured and displaced?
I need someone who will love me past my pain, shame and disgrace.

Someone who will feed into me because right now I feel empty with nothing left to give,
This pain has me struggling to breathe, questioning whether I want to live.
I am stuck in a dark place and I need someone to hold my hand during these moonless nights.
Someone who understands my pain and is an example that everything will be alright.
I am in need of much, I feel like I lost everything in one day,
The magnitude of this situation has me discombobulated and my thoughts in disarray.
One thing I do know, have learned, and understand,
Never allow your single, lonely friend any kind of access to your man!!!

Pulling Me Back

It is hard to move on when that certain someone insists on pulling you back
In my mind things may be over but their insistence to stay prevents things from fading to black
I am battling with the idea of staying put or leaving as I had originally intended.
All of these conflicting emotions arise when reconsidering a relationship that has been ended.
In the perfect world our situation would not have come to this.
We would be happy with no questions to contemplate or address.

It is really hard to move on when that certain someone continues to pull you back;
Especially when that someone momentarily sent your life off track.
It is never fun when you are caught in love's tug-of-war
You find yourself wanting to stay as you are walking out the front door.
Sometimes you are up, most of the time you are down.
Because there is a piece of you that questions if the one you love will consistently be around.

It is very hard to move on when that certain someone continues to pull you back.
There is an emotional conflict happening and your heart and mind are under attack.
You simply want to gain some peace, only wanting to know that love is here to stay.
But in love nothing is ever certain; it is just designed that way.
In love there is pain; pain that produces emotional setback.
It is what happens when that certain someone continues to pull you back.

Beats Being Nice

You are upset without reason; caught up in emotions that should not be. The more that I evaluate the situation I realized you are more upset with yourself than you are with me. Misery loves company and it is obvious that you are its best friend. I have grown tired of dealing with the little boy who sells himself as a man. I tried to stick by your side but it became obvious that you lack direction. You move as the wind blows; thirsty for attention. Erratic and unstable, I understand why you consistently fail in reaching the next plateau. It is impossible to grow maturity in an empty vessel? You do not know half of what you think you know. I will not call you a waste of time but it was time misspent. I am just thankful that I realized your insignificance before I fell into your malcontent. You truly leave me disgusted and saddened that I ever allowed you to be a part of my life. You are a poor example of a man; sometimes the truth beats being nice!

Farewell

I don't want him but for some reason you are convinced that I do. If I wanted him, he was there for the taking long before I met you. He is my friend, someone that I confide in when I need someone to talk to. He hears my heart during the times your pride won't allow you to. You have nothing to worry about; he is not the type of man who will disrespectfully cross the line. He respects the things that are his and those that are mines. Your insecurity in unwarranted, whatever you suspect is completely in your mind. There is no need for you to be watching me so closely; find something better to do with you time. If you cannot trust me then there is no need for you to be here. A relationship cannot prosper when attention to it is driven through fear. Most of what you feel is the guilt from your own actions. Trying to place blame on me serves only as a distraction; and I am not having it. So I will give you two options and this will be the only time that I say it. Get your act together or go play with those who allow you to play with them. I am not someone who will; I am far past the childish games. I refuse to engage in he say – she say or become the target of thirsty females and their derogatory claims. I am a self-assured woman and I do not need you for validation. You must understand that I will not accept being one of the women in your rotation. I reiterate that my male friends are not in my life to replace you;

even if this is not how you perceive it to be. Honestly, there is no need to replace you because eventually you will leave. You have not shown me that you can remain faithful and take care of home. I am beginning to see that I am better off being alone. I am not foolish nor am I buying what you are trying to sell; either you get your act together or I bid you farewell.

"What Man?"

As a child, I endured many years of uncertainty because he was not there. I sometimes wondered if he thought of me; if he even cared. I struggled to define what a man's love really was and in the process, I became discerning and calculated. I would never allow a man to hurt me; my views of them were already distorted and contaminated. Never really took a man seriously until I had established a life where there was no need for one. Figured I would get myself to a place where I would be ok if he decided to tuck his tail and run.

I thought I heard God tell me that this man was the one to whom I should marry but he ended up being the man I would carry. He did nothing but hurt my heart and rip open wounds that I thought had healed. Ran away like a coward and tried to portray me as the heel. My selfish ambition pushed me into a situation that lead nowhere. How do you flourish with a man who is not fully prepared? The enemy used him to prey upon my insecurity in an effort to destroy. Thought I was being blessed with a man who turned out to be nothing but a boy. Separation was forced from the pain of no longer wanting to try. Within the pain of failure, I learned that it was ok to cry. Rivers of disappointment flowed freely as internal cleansing commenced. I once again found my peace in asserting my independence. No gates to guard my heart, just separation from those with no aspiration. Before I say "I Do" ever again I will know the beast I am taking in.

Perspective

Words with no substance are empty. Why do they move you? Even in a moment of slander you can decide the outcome that you ultimately come to. It took me a long time to realize that I cannot control the variables; I can only control my perspective. No matter how many untruths that rain from the mouths of those who wish to see me fall, I never lose focus on my overall objective. Success will always come with opposition; this is the only way you come to appreciate victory. With this opposition come multiple lessons of true loyalty; however, that slope is slippery. You can never completely trust anyone with your entire story; everyone does not interpret what they read the same. This is how folks come to conclusions that misrepresent your character and dirty your name. In all things the truth has a way of making its way into the light. So hold your peace and maintain your focus in the midst of defamation; everything will be alright.

I Am Hurting

I want to cry but my heart is empty, I am unable to pour out emotion that is no longer there.
I want to scream to alleviate frustration and to wake myself from this nightmare.
My heart is empty; drained of love.
I no longer know the feeling; I am a shell of who I once was.
Existing; not living.
Unaware of space and time;
Neglecting all that requires me to feel; but I am fully aware of how love causes you to go blind.
I want to see happiness without the possibility of disappointment.
But my heart is empty; depleted by actions that were recklessly inconsistent.
I am a weak, hollowed vessel; forced to survive on a heart that faintly beats
How do I discover peace if this agony that I experience will never cease
I am left to ponder love because I am unable to feel.
Unable to differentiate between what is fake and what is real.
I now hurt those who cross my path; misery hates to be alone.
I have grown to realize; despair is simply misery's chaperone.
This emptiness that I have is the primary contributor to my pain.
Within my emptiness is a quietness that is steadily driving me insane.

I want to expel this despair and no longer allow emptiness to control my life.

How do I live my life in abundance if my heart is forever deprived?

My heart is empty but I want to experience love in complete fullness.

There is no lonelier feeling than loving someone who does not acknowledge that you exist.

Liberation

My ex almost broke me; mentally, physically, and emotionally.
He would constantly push me away instead of drawing me close, holding me.
He would call me names and tell me that I was nothing without him,
Often attacking me like a savage beast trying to dismantle its prey limb from limb.
I just wanted to be loved and appreciated; treated like a queen,
But his idea of affection was tearing me down and treating me mean.
I would try to talk to him to gain some type of understanding,
But my quest to understand only led to further misunderstanding.
I loved this man with everything within me,
But I was living life in hell and I needed to get free.
I knew it would not be easy because of his controlling nature,
But I had grown weary and I knew that I deserved better.
I packed my bags and left one day while he was away,
I had no place to go; there was no place for me to stay.
I found peace within my decision to step away and begin anew,
Nothing could be worse than the three years that I had just gone through.
For weeks, I moved from place to place in fear

that he was searching for me,
I knew if he caught up with me the kind of situation it would be.
I physically could not take the abuse anymore,
Mentally I was at my wits end; the emotional torment I could no longer ignore.
I kept moving; and my weeks turned into months and I slowly began to feel better about my situation,
I began to remember that there is a GOD bigger than these trials that I was facing.
One Sunday morning after jumping around from place to place I went to church and felt right at home,
A resting place, where I was shown that I no longer had to travel these empty roads alone;
God restored all that was stripped from me; no longer was I living in lack,
I now believed that I was strong enough to resist any temptation; fend off any attack.
I stopped running; no longer consumed with the spirit of fear.
My hurt washed away through prayer and the shedding of tears.
You have to understand the liberation that came from knowing that everything was going to be ok,
Sometimes the hardest thing to do when you are in hell is to believe that GOD will make a way.
Now equipped with a new sense of self and the Armor of GOD, I decided to hide no more,
GOD immediately tested my faith because the next day I ran into my ex at the grocery store.

When I first saw him I really was not sure of how to feel,
I felt like I literally stepped outside of myself; the situation was surreal.
He immediately walked up on me and started to talk down on me in an effort to break my will,
But I told him to respect my decision to leave and how it is I feel.
I politely kept it moving and he forcefully grabbed me as if I belonged to him,
I could not believe what was happening; I tell you the nerve of some men...
I told him to let me go or we would definitely have a serious problem;
That if he could not get his problems together that I would find someone to solve them.
I let him know that this is no longer about him but completely about me,
That I was once blinded by the fear of him but now I clearly see.
I went on to tell him that I would not allow another man to break my will or hurt me ever again,
That what he had done to me was real and it was on him to try to make amends.
I let him know that I had already forgiven him because it was my belief that he did not know what he had truly done,
But the fact of the matter was I had grown since then; quite frankly I was no longer the one.
I wished him the best and I calmly walked away,

Thank GOD for the strength to stand and for always making a way.

A Dream

Last night I awoke from a dream where I relived my heart's worst pain.
I am not sure why I had such a dream;
That part of the story is hard to explain.
What I do know is this was a dream that played out more like a nightmare. One so frightening that it sent me into immediate prayer...

Heavenly Father please take this pain from me; forever casting it away.
I no longer wish to feel love in this way.
My heart is faint; my will, much the same.
With thoughts of negativity afflicting my mind; I am not sure if I can sustain.
This burden I can no longer haul; I have carried it long enough.
Although my heart longs for it; letting go of love has become a must
Lord, I have been shaken and I am too fragile to be hurt once more.
I am hesitant to walk into love, only to be let down like before.
Lord, loose me from these restraints that hurt has placed upon my heart.
My faith in love has been crippled; paralyzing the beat of my heart.
I need a release from this agony; I yearn to once again know happiness in its fullness.
I would not wish for my enemy to have to experience this.
Please help me understand the reason for this

vision that reopened such a devastating wound.
I thought that I had made it through the pain that had so overwhelmingly consumed.
Lord, I ask you to make a way like only You can.
Now I lay me back down to sleep;
Praying for your peace and your comfort
AMEN

Second Look

Trouble does not last always; you just have to be strong enough to get through it.
Everything that does not feel right is not necessarily trouble; it all depends on how you view it.
You have no growth without first enduring the storm; it provides the water to your soul.
Although you sometimes feel like you are drowning, it is the water that nourishes and provides you strength to pull up and out of that dark hole.
It will never be easy but it is a struggle that builds character.
You usually only endure the same thing twice if GOD's lesson fails to register.
Learn how to be still and listen to GOD when storms are raging.
The crashing thunder serves merely as a distraction to prevent you from hearing what GOD is saying.
This is why it is important to diligently seek GOD, even before the storm comes.
Take solice in knowing that the battle is not yours; you have already won.
It is only when we fail to fully know the TRUTH that we allow doubt to creep into our minds and test our faith.
This doubt gives the devil room to operate; but I decree, in your life the devil has no place!
Continue to press towards the mark in all that you do; this is only the beginning.
Never hang your head even when it looks like

you are not winning.
Remember prayer changes things; GOD always has a ram in the bush.
My advice to you would be, after you pray, to always take a second look.

My Loss, My Gain

GOD works in mysterious ways and my faith in HIM allows me to face this test with the assurance that something greater is coming later.
Still I feel the pain of losing my unborn child; it's only human nature.
My heart was ready to love; my body was beginning to go through changes,
Now with my healing at the forefront, I am rediscovering happiness in stages.
I had great expectations; excitement on cloud nine.
But GOD had different plans and decided that it just was not my time.
So now I deal with a loss that is more personal than anything I have ever come up against,
I am trying to understand what happened, trying to make it make sense.
I did everything right; I took my prenatal vitamins and made sure that I stayed away from being stressed.
BUT GOD felt that before I became a mother there are some things with me that still needed to be addressed.
So I sit here with no questions; only the assurance that motherhood is soon to come.
This too is but a test.
How do I know?
I reflect upon all of the many trials HE has brought me from.
This load is not too heavy; after all I don't carry it alone.

I have a great man in my life and together we will take this life experience and use it as a stepping stone.
My mind is tranquil; my heart is not burdened with grief.
I am more than a conqueror and GOD grants me peace.

As These Tears Flow

As these tears flow...
I can feel the pain subside. After years of torment and shame I can no longer hold this pain inside. I'm letting it all go; putting my frustrations in the hands of the Lord. No longer willing to accept the ramifications of past relationships filled with so much strife and discord. Once I am all cried out, the pain that floods my soul will be no more. GOD said it is finished; now I'm preparing to be blessed like never before.

As these tears flow...
I realize that I have walked this road for far too long, blaming myself for relationships that did not work. Repeatedly, allowing myself to experience such tantalizing hurt. I was confused. In my eagerness to move away from my past I further enhanced my malcontent. So in essence I am to blame for much of my discontent.

As these tears flow...
I can taste the bitterness that grew to shape and define my disposition. The same bitterness that closed my mind and shut down my heart; feeding my refusal to listen.

It is a taste that I had to acquire to somehow numb the pain. But it was in this same bitterness that I found much disdain

As these tears flow...
My vision is made clear. I am beginning to see that part of what was holding me back was fear. The fear of how I would be perceived by the next man to come into my life. But fear only kept me from again experiencing happiness; not from being hurt twice. The Lord did not give me the spirit of fear. So now it is time for me to depart from here

As these tears flow...
I am crying the river that will wash me clean. Although I have subjected myself to much of it, I have to remember that I am a queen. GOD is providing revelation so that I can see myself as HE has created me to be. Trials and tribulations of the heart are a part of the revelation that will ultimately set me free. I'm learning that it is in my heartbreak that I am learning how to love. How I must honor and respect the matters of the heart even when no one else does. I have gained priceless wisdom that is raising me to a new plateau. But first I must allow these tears to flow...

Mother

Mother abandoned me and left me to fend for myself long before my adolescence.
Leaving me with this lonely feeling; yearning for her presence.
Many nights I cried for her, not receiving an answer or reply.
Where did Mother go? How could she leave me and never say goodbye?
Was it something that I did that caused her to turn and walk away?
A mother's love for her child is not displayed in this way.
I have countless questions and not one answer; how do I cope with these issues that have been left unaddressed?
My story is depicted by a wordless book; once you get past the cover there is nothing else.
I cannot escape this pain; my reflection bears the image of the woman who gave me life.
A constant reminder that I'm missing an integral part of my life
As a matter of fact, nothing is right at all.
I feel like Mother let me down when she allowed me to fall.
I was her only girl; and she chose to leave me as prey to this cruel world.
So where do I go from here; how do I find my identity?
I want to escape this hell and find some peace and serenity.
I am tired of this pain; I often wish Mother would have given her rejection upon

conception.
Then I would not be here with this feeling, I would not have to worry about why Mother created this disconnection.
I cry daily, tears are the only indication of my pain
I even cry in my sleep; constant weeping has left my pillows stained.
I cry out to GOD hoping that HE hears my plea.
All I truly want in life is for Mother to come back to me.

Her Story, Her Reality

There is a story behind a very promiscuous woman. She craves the attention of men who will lead her to destruction. Unable to abstain from sexual behavior; she cannot help that she has become a slave to her past. Every time she tries to do better she thinks back and her progress is instantly halted! She is moving nowhere fast. But she has a story and what you don't know is she was sexually abused from the age of six until she moved away from home. Her daddy was a sick bastard that would touch her in places that needed to be left alone. For twelve years, he sexually exploited her and manipulated her mind; leading her to believe that his abuse was really love. So when he let her go out into the world his vile and cruel acts against her formed her thinking and the attitude that she still has not been able to break free of. Her daddy destroyed her; he never gave her a chance. Sex is the only form of affection that she has ever received from a man. So, do not blame her for her actions; no one ever showed her how a man should properly love a woman. All she can remember from her past is her father's abuse, silent cries, insides swollen. Because of this she will never be able to bare children or know the joys of maternity. This was not her choice; to have her pleasure and pain share the same identity. Now in her mind she needs sex and these thoughts are hard for her to resist. She is simply driven by a sickness and a past that causes her to act like this. She is a very promiscuous woman but you cannot judge her if you have not felt her pain. If you do anything, help her discover who and what she could be instead of trying to be the next man to ride her train. This is her story, this is her reality; Actions birthed from a childhood of manipulation and brutality.

Before I Surrender

I have had my fair share of men; it is not necessarily something I am proud of. There were many years where I was lost in search of a certain kind of love. I put myself in situations to be used because I was unsure of what to demand. I was so consumed with having somebody that I dated young boys hoping that they could operate as men. I gave of myself; finding myself empty and unfulfilled. After dealing with so many fakes; I found it hard to tell what was real. Now to keep from diminishing my self-worth I keep away from those who have nothing to bring to the table. No I am not a gold-digger but I want to know that whomever I choose to be with is ready, willing, and able. I have wasted too much time investing in those that did not deserve me. So now I make sure he will do all the things to secure me. That means treating me with respect; every lady deserves that much. Always a gentleman; not so quick to try and touch. Opens my doors and pulls out my chairs. Rooted in the Word; taking all directions from the MAN upstairs. Swag on ten and his style sophisticated and polished. Educated in various ways; he graduated from the streets before he received a degree from college. Loves his momma; after God, family is front and center. This is the kind of man I want before I decide to surrender.

The Difference

Never be so quick to cling to a man just because he shows you something new. If he is the man in your life he should make it his business to impress you. Don't be fooled by first impressions; what you see thereafter is what matters most. Every man will tell you that they are the best thing for you; it is in a man's nature to brag and boast. Remember he is trying to impress you; be slow to show that you are intrigued by his presentation. Pay attention to his actions; do not allow what you hear to get lost in translation. Every man has a goal and most of the time it is not you. It is what resides in between your thighs and he has every intention of breaking through. So yes, he will say what needs to be said and he will do what needs to be done; all in an effort to have a little sexual fun. As a woman, it is your job to create a situation that will make a man work on levels where he is not familiar. When presented with such a task a man will either; tuck his tail and run or stand and deliver. Men who only seek physical satisfaction usually do not have the mental strength required to think under pressure; they typically break. However, a man who is ready will be able to connect with you on all levels, see you through fresh eyes, speak to you in a steady voice and physically demonstrate. Actions speak louder than words and the eyes never lie. A trained mind helps in knowing when to bring them in or when to tell them goodbye. Out of love I tell you this in hopes that clarity is brought to the forefront of your mind. Delicate flowers are easily bruised and deterred when scorned continually over long periods of time. I ask that you be slow to anger as I reveal to you the truth even if it is not pleasing to your ears. The truth is never pleasant when it addresses your short-comings and your fears. The truth is; you are selling yourself short by staying connected to a man who does not love you. Your inability to move shows that you are weak and willing to endure whatever hell he chooses to take you through. You believe that if you pray; GOD will remove you from the situation with your heart unaffected. You are failing to use wisdom; allowing less to become your standard, while leaving yourself unprotected. Your excuse is that you are not built to walk away; he must leave you instead. Your foolishness is more than likely why he chose you; your vulnerability causes you to be easily led. You agreed to be something that he does; you are merely a change of pace. Now faced with the truth you cower in the midst of your disgrace. You choose to close your eyes to his demeaning acts; unable to confront your feebleness. Yet, somehow you believe your blessing will come before the situation is fully addressed. Deliverance will only come when you learn to assert your independence. Until then, happiness and pain share the same space; leaving you unable to tell the difference.

Courting a Woman

You want to come over?!?
What do you mean you want to come over?!?
Why can't we go out on a date?!?
And why is it that every time you call it is far too late?
I hope that you do not think that I am going to let you come watch Netflix and chill; I can do that alone.
I am not going to allow any random man to enter my home.
You should not want to come over anyway; you should be more concerned with showing me why I should keep you around.
Your actions thus far are the reason that most men get turned down.

No, I do not wish to come to your house; that is no better than you coming to mine.
Why are we having this discussion via text message; have you lost your mind? You are so impersonal; how am I supposed to know if I like you if we never have an adult conversation.
I am far too grown to allow myself to engage in such childish communication.
It is impossible to court a woman and not be present!
Nothing can be realized in relationship until quality time is spent.
This cannot be done by sitting on the couch having a text message conversation.
Women want to see a man outside in the

elements to see how he reacts to a variety of situations.
And men wonder why we do them the way that we do.
There is no need to be courteous when all a man really wants to do is get in bed with you.

Can You Blame Her?

I am just a bit flustered by how weak some men can be.
They would rather be entrapped by the scandalous ways of someone no good than to find freedom in the respect and values of a lady.
Does the challenge a lady presents change the perspective from which a man approaches the situation?
I say absolutely!!!
Some men choose to read the book with the fewest words and the most animation.
Less work is enticing; especially when less work still produces the desired outcome.
The fact that you are a lady and better overall does not play in your favor; the easiest road is usually chosen when it is all said and done.
Some ladies fall victim to this trend and lower their standards to become a part of the game.
A boy does not know how to treat a lady accordingly and lowering your standard leaves you partly to blame.
Now due to the inability of some men to be a man, ladies have begun to shut down to the notion that good men still exist.
When presented with a good man it causes a woman to question "What manner of man is this?"
I shake my head in disappointment at the realization that a woman must question the willingness and sincerity of a true King; a man who knows and performs his duties in a

prestigious manner.
But due to the current state of things; tell me...
Can You Blame Her?

Play Your Position

It is a dangerous thing to make a request when you are not ready for it to come into fruition. Sometimes it is better to keep your peace and play your position. The grass is not always greener on the other side. So do not get all in your feelings when you find out the truth and it damages your pride. Do not spin your story and try to place blame where it does not belong. We can be our own worst enemy; you sat yourself out of your own home. Reality will chastise you when you accept fantasy as truth; especially when that truth is rooted in the ignorance of your youth. Maturity does not constitute separation it simply provides perspective. However; when you mishandle what has been shown to you it will more than likely leave you hurt and very reflective. Now you are on the outside looking in and you feel like I did you bad. Blind man, what continues to be your mistake is your inability to realize the greatness that you had. I may have not been all that you desired but I was everything that you stood in need of. Now you must deal with emptiness that comes from stepping away from your one true love.

Catch Up

You have to work for this;
I am not easy nor will I ever allow any man to devalue me.
I am appalled that you would have the audacity to approach me as if I would sleep with you just because you have a little money. And I stress... A LITTLE MONEY!!!
I have been a boss; my money still has the green hue
I am still spending currency acquired before they sucked the life out of Benjamin and turned him blue.
I seriously thought of smacking some sense into you; I do not do well with disrespect.
And just so you know, you could not have gotten any of this even if you had come at me correct!
I know your type and you are not ready for a lady of my stature.
I would put something on you so serious that you would have gotten caught up in the rapture.
You young boys kill me portraying yourselves as men but have no clue how to engage a lady in decent conversation.
How do you ever expect to get a woman if you cannot even gain her attention?
I am so disappointed in your presentation, pissed off at your attempt.
You are the perfect example of why, for most men, I have such discontent.
Get it together and get lost; find yourself

someone else to aggravate.
Your immaturity leaves you countless dollars short and infinite days late.
It is time to CATCH UP!!

In This Moment

On this late night, we sit in a warm bubble bath;
Rose petals, Patron and candle light.
The ambiance of the moment has me thankful to GOD for blessing me with someone who knows how to love me right.
Gently, he rubs my body and the tension within begins to fade away.
There is something special about a man who knows how to touch you the right way.
He started out by rubbing the back of my neck; which sent a tingling sensation down to my toes.
His touch sent my body into total submission; I still remember the scent of strawberry rose
He continued to rub descending down to my shoulders; rubbing so deep that I could feel the effects in the small of my back;
I was left completely paralyzed; there is not much you can do when a man knows how to touch you like that!!!
His hands then roamed freely down my arms until he reached my hands, our fingers interlocked.
I was so caught up in him touching my body that I didn't want him to stop.
If the water had cooled down, the heat of our bodies spiked the temperature up.
It is amazing the way that the body responds to the simplest of touch.
As he wrapped his arms around me and held me close he began to kiss me gently.

I had never felt this way; I am lost in his love.
In this moment, he is showing me love in ways I have never known
I am grateful that I have moved from boys to men; from childish ways to actions that are grown.

An Experience

Real women no longer seek sex, we are after an experience.
If all women ever wanted was a quickie, we could do that for ourselves and not be inconvenienced.
Women are tired of two pumps and a slow grind representing the climax of something that was supposed to be much more.
Ladies are in search of a man that will make love to them, not treat them like they are a whore.
A man's imagination gives him the opportunity to fulfil a woman's fantasy;
To gratify a woman's wildest thoughts before he ever moves to please her sexually.
I am speaking of a series of situations that leave lasting sensations that later lead to late-night expressions.
Moments where the culmination feels more like appreciation rather than a two-minute demonstration.

Make Me Want to Love You

Make me want to love you; nothing ever happens just because.
Give me a reason to fall deeply in love.
We have similarities; a personal desire to be loved and to love in return; but in no way are our similarities my chief concern.
I want to be persuaded; convinced without a shadow of a doubt that love has come and consumed me entirely.
I am speaking of a love so strong that it uplifts, fortifies, and inspires me.
I want to be pressed into submission by a love that is stronger than any barrier that heartbreak has placed in the way.
A love that is continuously evident in your walk and in your talk; never ceasing to be on display.
I want you to love me as GOD loves the church; unwavering in your commitment.
This is the only way that you can come to live in my heart and maintain permanent residence.
Speak to my heart because my ears have fallen deaf to the commonality of general conversation.
I need you to go deeper; speak to my love through muted vocalization.
Words with no sound, conveyed through actions bold and profound.
I want you to go deeper; allow your good deeds to become repetitious; more truth; less fictitious.

Reveal the answers to a love that is all too obscure and mysterious.
Make me love you; leave me no choice but to comply with your every request.
Bring me a happiness that causes me to say YES to everything you suggest.
I am not implying I will take on a servant's attitude and become feeble and weak.
I am merely suggesting that I want my actions to be induced by the feelings that are conduced only when our minds meet.

A Good Thing

I am a little old fashioned in my thinking; I believe a man should propose to a woman. There can be no greater feeling than the man of your dreams getting on bended knee and asking if he could have the honor of being your husband. Although times have changed and women have become more assertive in how they approach men concerning marriage. I believe that a man's proposal to a woman is a moment that is lasting and should forever be cherished. I mean no disrespect to those women who feel its ok to propose to a man. To me that goes directly against GOD's design; it was never a part of the original plan. In our day and age men feel great pressure to battle a woman's past while being her present. So why burden him with marriage before it is truly meant? This is not to say that you don't make yourself known to your man, he needs to know your expectations and your desires for your life. I haven't met one REAL man who didn't want to one day have a beautiful woman as his wife. When GOD says, it is time HE will put it upon a man's heart to go out and get that diamond ring. For a man who finds a wife finds a good thing!

I Am Afraid

I am afraid; I have been here a time or two and things have never ended well. Every time I have given my heart to a man, he has let me down, hurt me, flat-out failed. But I see you and I am elated by the possibilities of what could be. You have my attention; you have arrested my thoughts and I am not sure if I want them set free. Still, within this excitement rest an uneasiness that I cannot escape. Although pieces of you have already infiltrated my heart, I am not sure how much of you I can take. I am afraid; no one has been able to love my heart after they have obtained it; no one has ever dared to claim it. I am fearful that you may do the same, hence my reluctance to commit. I apologize if it sounds like I am putting you in a box with those who came before but I must be careful with my heart. My love is the greatest thing that I have to offer and before I turn it over to you I have to be sure that you have the characteristics that set you apart. Nothing about right now is a game to me; I want you; I feel it every time we are in one another's presence. But I want to be clear that this is not just about unfiltered lust and more about pure essence. The basic, real, and invariable nature of love and all of its expressive elements; Infused with the qualities that radiates validity and relevance. But I am afraid…Have I become a hollow defensive shell that can no longer give? Are my insecurities the overwhelming factor in the decisions that I make? Has love escaped me although I have endlessly pursued its infectious embrace? I am afraid; I still remember the tears flowing uncontrollably from my eyes while asking myself why I always choose the devil in disguise. My heart bled for many moons but as I healed this fear set in. Please forgive me if I hold you at bay; in many ways, my heart has yet to mend. I ask that you show me who you are and allow your righteousness to push out those things that have left me unwilling move. Show me your love so that I am no longer afraid.

The Privilege

Sexual encounters are dangerous undertakings when viewed as miniscule. Underestimating the power of human emotion is the precursor to inevitable heartbreak. Foolishly mishandling lustful desires causes you to make your temple accessible. Once you allow all that is sacred to be interrupted by acts of fornication; all innocence passes away. In your urgency to satisfy a momentary impulse you accepted emotional turmoil. A connection established by gross impartation. He now inhabits you in ways that cannot be perceived with human eyes. He occupies a part of your spirit that only arises when your hormones begin to rage. You blindly make him an acquaintance who serves as the instigator to a sexual appetite that once lay dormant. The damage that has been inflicted strips you of that which was purposed for someone who would love and appreciate you. There is no taking back what has already been mindlessly given away.

He Cares

I want to know that he cares. Can he say good morning as the sun rises and good night when the moon shines? He does not have to stay in my DM's but I want to know that he aspires to be mines. I have made it to the level where the little things mean more than a few dollars ever could. I now understand that it takes much more to build a house than good wood. I am evolving; and with maturity comes greater responsibility and demonstration. I am just not a part of the moment I am participating. I am going to make my presence felt by doing the things that are desired and required. And just when you think you are tired I will dig into my bag of tricks and leave you inspired. I'm done playing games with those who lack the potential to win. I am done trying to be a girlfriend I want to become your next of kin. The one who gets the ring and is placed before your mother. No disrespect to your mother but she cannot love you under the covers. As your wife, I can and I will give that much and more. Couch, bed, shower, and even on the floor. But I have to be the one; not just one of a chosen few. I am one in a million, not the one you play with but the one that you pursue.

www.ingramcontent.com/pod-product-compliance
Lightning Source LLC
Chambersburg PA
CBHW060430050426
42449CB00009B/2216